SHAPE UP!

David A. Adler

illustrated by Nancy Tobin

Holiday House / New York

Library of Congress Cataloging-in-Publication Data

Adler, David A.

Shape Up! Fun with triangles and other polygons / by David A. Adler;
illustrated by Nancy Tobin. — 1st ed.

p. cm.

Summary: Uses cheese slices, pretzel sticks, a slice of bread,
graph paper, a pencil, and more to introduce various polygons, flat
shapes with varying numbers of straight sides.

ISBN 0-8234-1346-2 (hardcover)

1. Geometry — Juvenile literature. [1. Geometry.] I. Tobin,
Nancy, III. II. Title

QA445.5.A35 1998

516'.15—dc21   97-22236

CIP

AC

What is a POLYGON?

**It's a flat shape
with all straight sides.**

Now,
that's what I
call a
square meal!

With two slices of American cheese, a toothpick,
pretzel sticks, plain paper, graph paper, a pencil,
a plastic knife, and a slice of bread
you can learn
more about them.

You can also eat if you get hungry!

TRIANGLES

Put a slice of American cheese on a plate.

With the tip of a toothpick, poke three small holes in the cheese. The holes should not be in a line. With the edge of the toothpick, cut the cheese by connecting the holes with three straight lines.

You have made a flat, three-sided figure – a cheese triangle.

Triangles are three-sided polygons.

Make another cheese triangle.
Do they look the same?
They probably don't.

While all triangles are closed shapes with three straight sides,
not all triangles are the same.

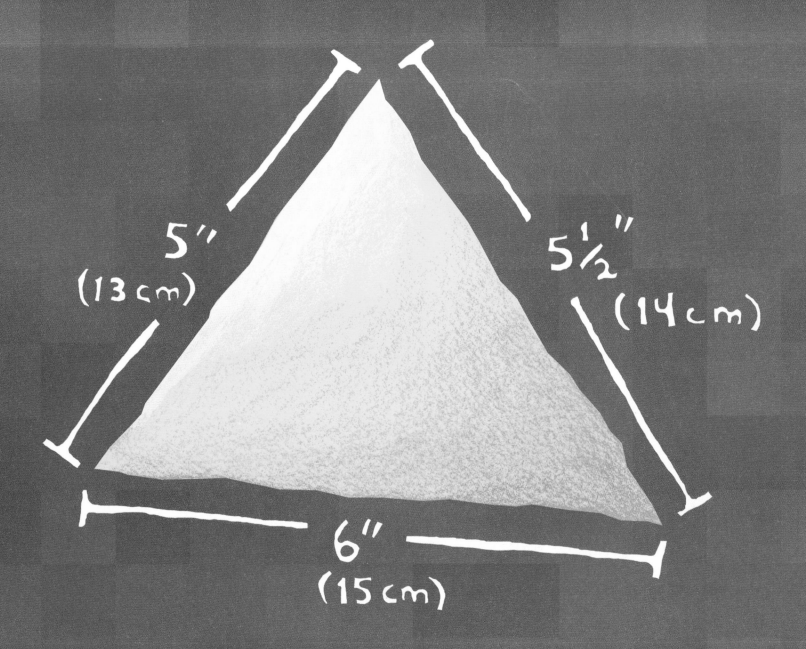

5" (13 cm)

5½" (14 cm)

6" (15 cm)

Look at either one of your cheese triangles.
Is every side a different length?
If every side is a different length,
your cheese triangle is a <u>scalene</u> triangle.

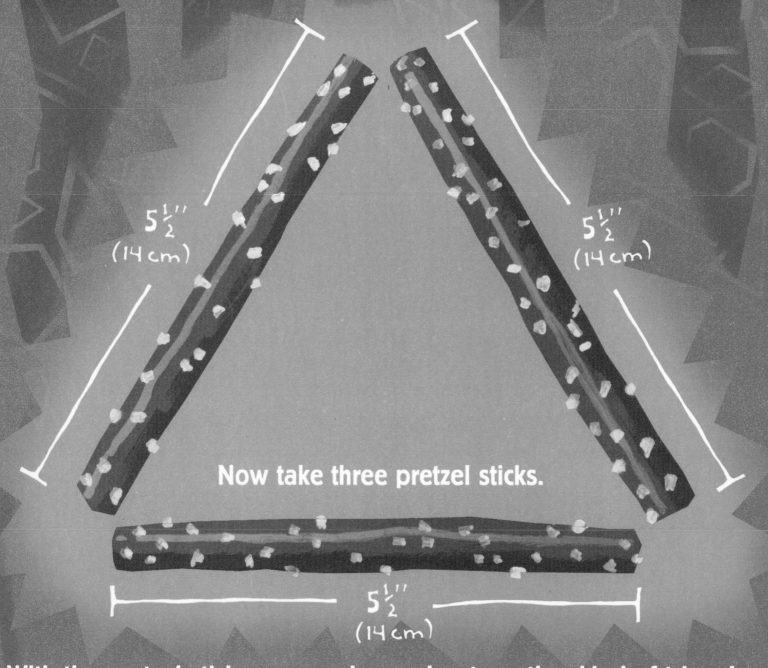

$5\frac{1}{2}''$
(14 cm)

$5\frac{1}{2}''$
(14 cm)

Now take three pretzel sticks.

$5\frac{1}{2}''$
(14 cm)

With the pretzel sticks you can learn about another kind of triangle.
Arrange the pretzels with the ends touching so they form a triangle.
Since each pretzel stick is the same length,
each side of the triangle is the same.
A triangle with three equal sides is an <u>equilateral</u> triangle.

Now take a bite
of one pretzel stick.
Arrange the
half-eaten pretzel
and two remaining
pretzel sticks
to form a triangle.

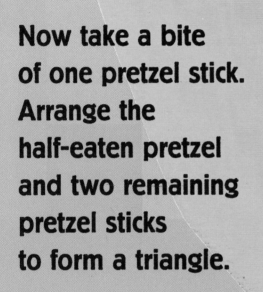

You have made a triangle
with just two equal sides.
You have made an
<u>isosceles</u> triangle.

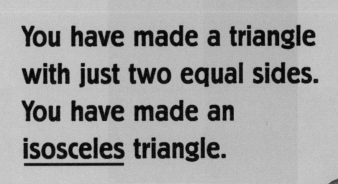

The sides of a triangle determine if it is a scalene, isosceles, or equilateral triangle.
The angles of a triangle also determine what kind of triangle it is.

Take two pretzel sticks.
Place them on a flat surface,
not in a line,
so the end of one pretzel
touches the end of the other.
The other ends
should not touch.

The two pretzels form an angle.
Each pretzel is one side, or arm, of the angle.
The point where the pretzel sticks
meet is the <u>vertex</u> of the angle.

Put your finger on the vertex. Hold it there.
Now move the other ends of the pretzel sticks
farther apart.

The angle is getting larger. Move the ends closer together.
Now the angle is getting smaller.

Now get a round sheet of paper.
Fold the paper once
so it has a straight edge.

Fold the paper again
so one half
of the straight edge
falls on top of the other.

RIGHT ANGLE

Where the two
straight edges meet,
they form an angle,
a <u>right</u> angle.

Draw some triangles on a sheet of paper.

Do you
see my
point?

Each triangle has three angles.

Use your paper right angle to measure
the angles of the triangles you drew.
If any angle you measure is also a right angle,
that triangle is a <u>right</u> triangle.

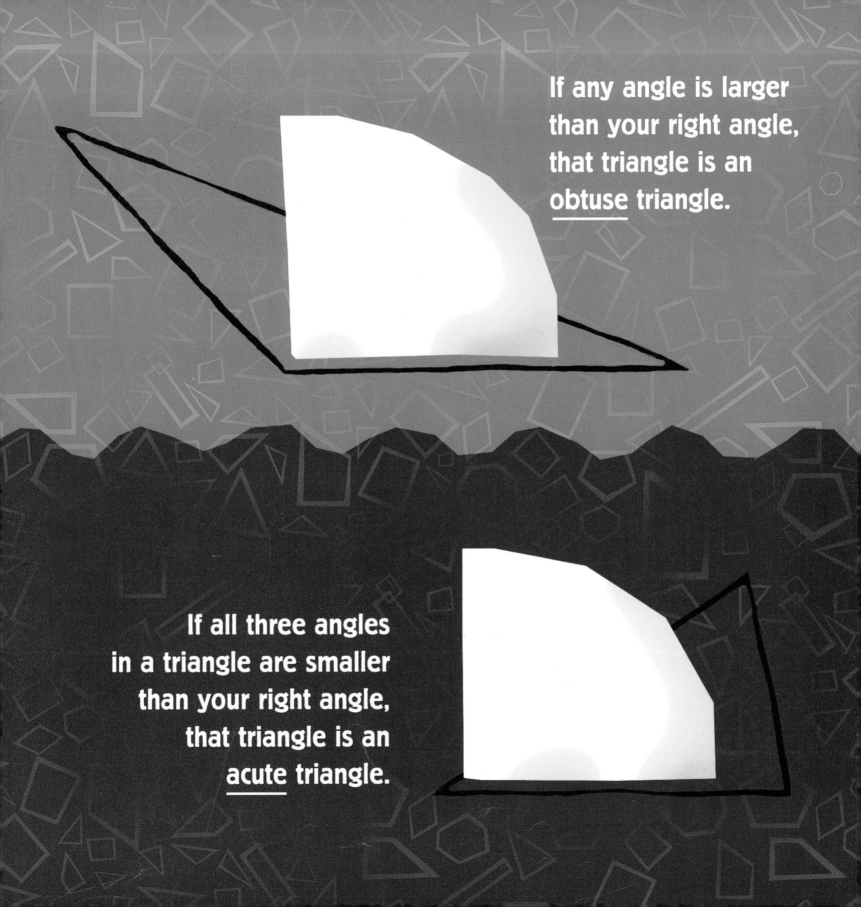

If any angle is larger than your right angle, that triangle is an **obtuse** triangle.

If all three angles in a triangle are smaller than your right angle, that triangle is an **acute** triangle.

QUADR

Now make four dots
anywhere on a sheet of paper, but not in a line.
Connect the dots with straight lines
to form a four-sided closed figure.

You have drawn a quadrilateral.

LATERALS

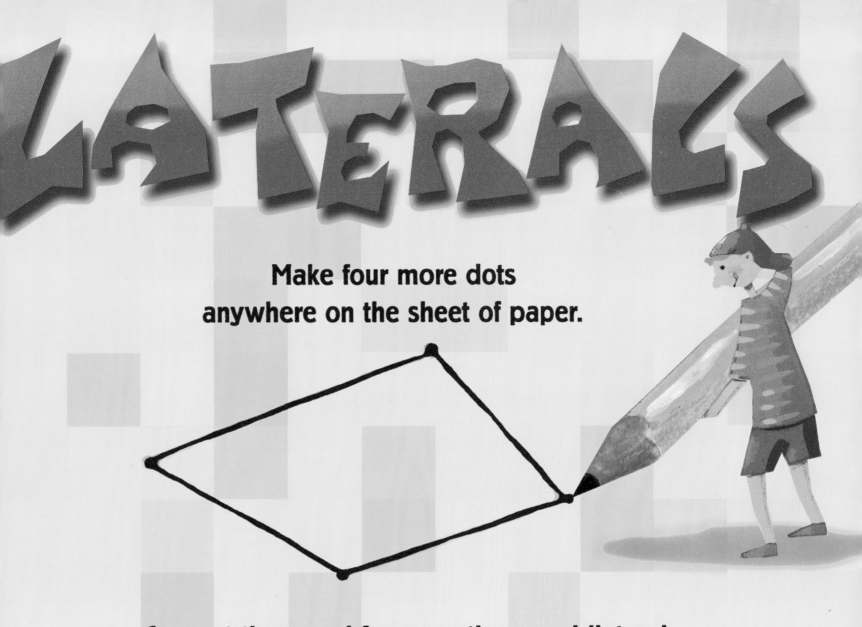

Make four more dots
anywhere on the sheet of paper.

Connect them and form another quadrilateral.
Do they look the same?
They probably don't.

While all quadrilaterals are closed shapes with four straight sides,
not all quadrilaterals are the same.

Using graph paper you can learn more about quadrilaterals.

There are two kinds of lines on the graph paper.

HORIZONTAL

There are horizontal – across – lines,

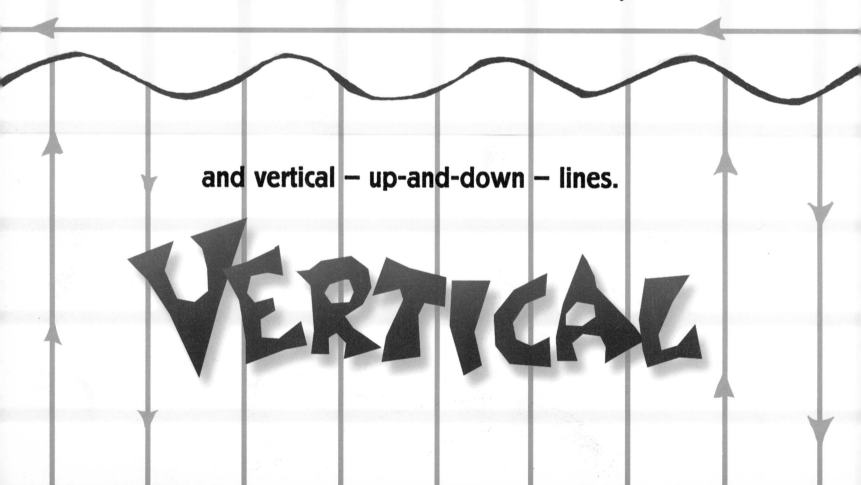

and vertical – up-and-down – lines.

VERTICAL

**Each horizontal line is parallel
with every other horizontal line on the page.
There is always the same distance between them.**

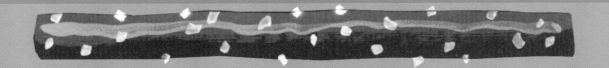

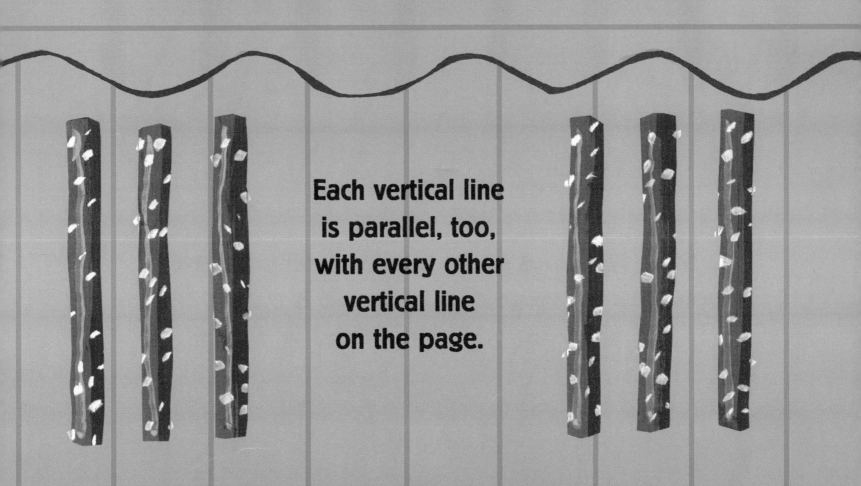

**Each vertical line
is parallel, too,
with every other
vertical line
on the page.**

Make two separate dots on one horizontal line.
Then, on another horizontal line,
make two separate dots a little farther apart from the first pair.
Connect the dots and draw a quadrilateral.

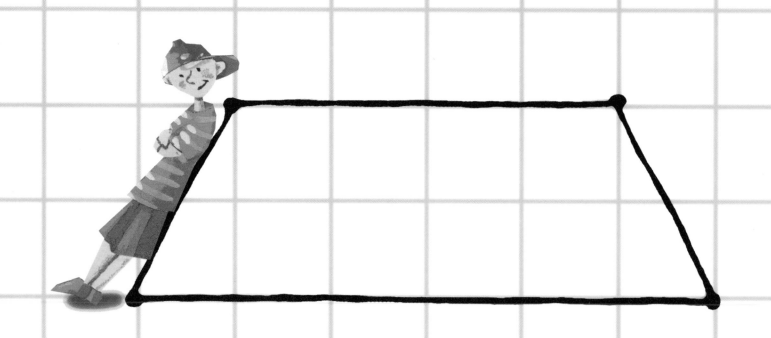

Since two sides of the quadrilateral are parallel,
you drew a <u>trapezoid</u>. A trapezoid is a quadrilateral
in which just one pair of sides is parallel.

A quadrilateral in which both pairs of opposite sides are parallel is a <u>parallelogram</u>.

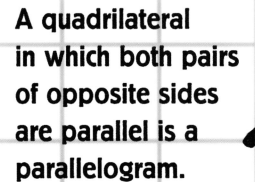

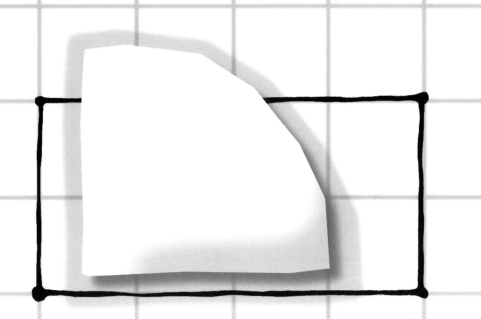

Here is a special kind of parallelogram.
Use your paper right angle to measure its angles.
Each should be a right angle.
It's a <u>rectangle</u>, a quadrilateral with four right angles.

Take four pretzel sticks
and arrange them with the
ends touching to form
a quadrilateral without
right angles.
Each pretzel stick
is the same length,
so each side of the
quadrilateral is the same.

You've made a <u>rhombus</u>,
a quadrilateral
with four equal sides.

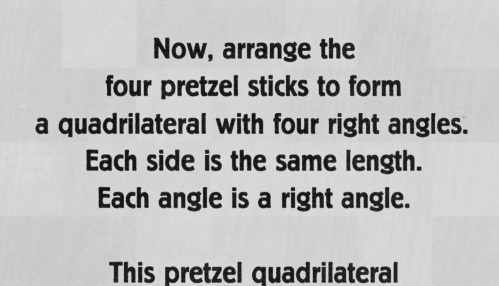

Now, arrange the
four pretzel sticks to form
a quadrilateral with four right angles.
Each side is the same length.
Each angle is a right angle.

This pretzel quadrilateral
is a <u>square</u>.

Look at your pretzel square.
Its opposite sides are parallel,
so it's a parallelogram, too.
Each angle is a right angle,
so it's a rectangle, too.

A square is a
quadrilateral with
four equal sides
and four
right angles.

Other POLYGONS

Now, take a slice of bread.
With a plastic knife,
trim the slice so it has
four straight sides.
It's in the shape of a
quadrilateral.

Cut a corner off.

Now the bread has five sides.
A five-sided polygon is a
pentagon.

Cut off another corner.

Now it has six sides.
A six-sided polygon is a hexagon.

Cut off another corner.

Now it has seven sides.
A seven-sided polygon is a
<u>heptagon</u>.

Now, that's a
shape I definitely
know!

Cut off the last corner.

Now it has eight sides.
An eight-sided polygon
is an <u>octagon</u>.

If you really like playing with your food, keep going!

A nine-sided polygon is a <u>nonagon</u>.

A ten-sided polygon is a <u>decagon</u>.

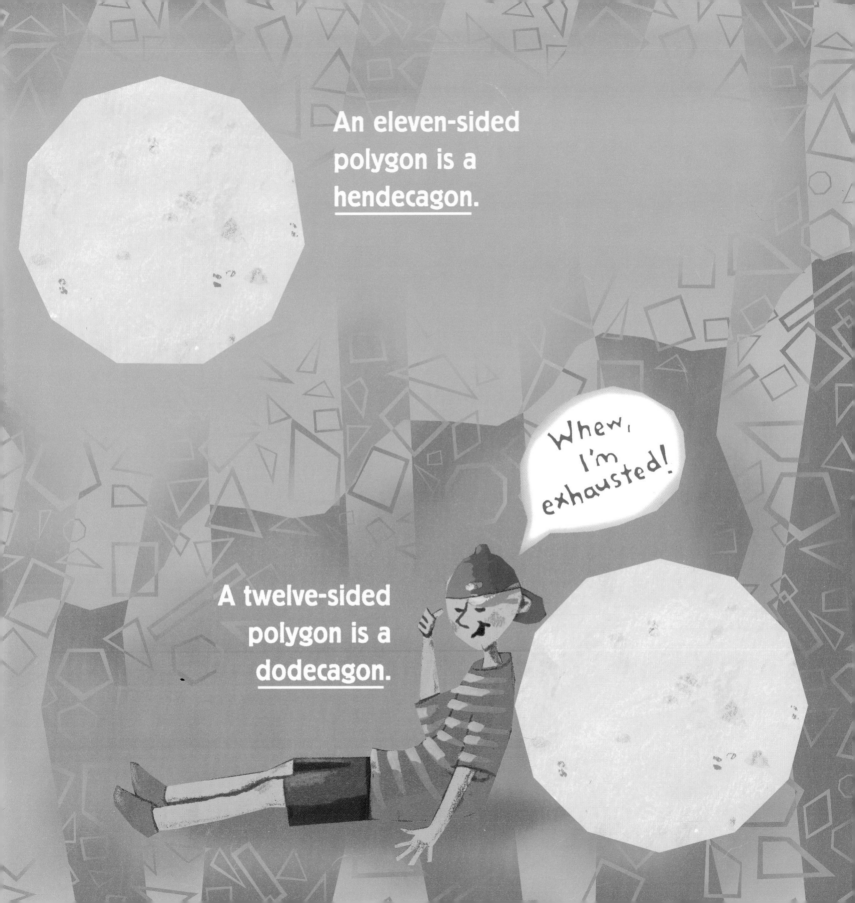

Look in your kitchen for polygon-shaped things.
Look in your classroom, too.
Keep on the lookout for polygons.

Triangles

scalene triangle
a triangle with unequal sides
equilateral triangle
a triangle with equal sides
isosceles triangle
a triangle with just two equal sides

Polygons

triangle
a three-sided polygon
quadrilateral
a four-sided polygon
pentagon
a five-sided polygon
hexagon
a six-sided polygon
heptagon
a seven-sided polygon
octagon
an eight-sided polygon
nonagon
a nine-sided polygon
decagon
a ten-sided polygon
hendecagon
an eleven-sided polygon
dodecagon
a twelve-sided polygon

Angles

right angle
an angle of 90 degrees
acute angle
an angle of less than 90 degrees
obtuse angle
an angle of more than 90 degrees
vertex
the point where two sides
of an angle meet

Quadrilaterals

trapezoid
a quadrilateral with just one pair
of parallel sides
parallelogram
a quadrilateral in which both pairs
of opposite sides are parallel
rectangle
a quadrilateral with four right angles
rhombus
a quadrilateral with four equal sides
and no right angles
square
a quadrilateral with
four equal sides and
four right angles